T0170154

LARA RAINS AND COLONIAL RITES

HOWARD A. FERGUS

LARA RAINS AND COLONIAL RITES

PEEPAL TREE

First published in Great Britain in 1998
Peepal Tree Press
17 King's Avenue
Leeds LS6 1QS
England

ISBN 0 94883 95 5

FOR CORETTA, COLIN AND CARLA

ACKNOWLEDGEMENTS

Some of these poems have originally appeared in *The Caribbean Writer* (USVI), *Caribanthology 2*, *Tower Poetry* (Canada), *Arts Review* (UWI) and *The Montserrat Reporter*

CONTENTS

Lara Rains	9
Lara Reach	10
BC Lara	11
Not Exactly Cricket	13
For Mandela	14
Jim Allen	15
Short of a Century	17
Death of a Friend	18
Barbados Medley	19
Columbus Poem	21
Ultimate	22
Holocaust	23
Private	24
Royal Garden Party	26
Mugged	28
For King and Colony	29
Toasted Majesty	31
Behind God Back	35
Imported Speech	37
Instead of Snow	39
Virgin Gorda	41
Caribbean Unity	43
Lament for Maurice Bishop	45
Informal	47
Damnick	48
Timo	50
Back then the Horse	52
At Grammar School	54
Graduation Fever	56
When Justice Came to Church	58
Tamarind Tree at St. Anthony's	59
Easter	60
Don't Blame God	61
Grave Beauty	62

You was a Freedom Fighter, Ma   63
Beetle   65
Prejudice   66
Love Birds   67
Love's Economy   68
Wife Poem   69
Third Birthday   70
Puberty   71
Early Morning Exercise   72
Meaning   74
Remembrance   75
Hurricane Romance   76
In Hugo Memoriam (1994)   77
Luis Passed   78
Bible on the Hill   80
Eclipse   81
The New Wave   83
Heights   84
At Fifty-five   85
Aging   87
At Cover   88
Gold Watch   89

NOTES   90

LARA RAINS

The rain stood still above Antigua
To watch Brian Lara flail and cut them
Over and over with a blunt willow
He buried them under a ruin of runs
In an Antiguan graveyard.
Inflating his countrymen, an absentee planter
Kissed Lara with 50 pieces sterling.

Playing with six stones
Like a broken rosary, two ombudsmen
Six feet deep in black and white
Performed last rites calling 'over and out'.

Digging their hell with a golden blade
Lara struck a jackpot among the shards
Where England sleeps, and raised both hands
In the shape of victory.
Mourners beat drums, drank deep
And a dirge of conch shells kept faith
For an uncertain resurrection
After 375 years of rain under Lara.

But the sun will not set
On the united state of the West Indies
And rain will come again.

LARA REACH

Lara jus reach
jus reach to de crease
and he reach century aready

Me here all de while
jus a blot jus a blot
jus a blot up mi piage with singles and dots

Lara settle and shuffle
he eye like a hawk
he leggo de bat firs ball, four, aff de mark

Me fire and miss
me miss like a piston dat sick,
a heart outa rhyddim; ball jus miss me right stick

Me put arn me helmet
me still a get hit
a get hit from de bounce of de bullet

Dey say me a run short
a run short of breath
me bound to get caught, caught out of me depth

De high-handed umpire
stick me up wid wan finger
wan wutless finger out me short of me number

Lara jus reach
jus reach to de crease
and he reach lord aready

BC LARA

Lara! Lara!
Lara! Lara!
Stop press pause time
voices swelled
like a Caribbean current
tossing its mane
driven by dancing winds
turning the tide of history
at Brian Lara's watershed
We shall build a new temple
for the sun and date time
from the year of Lara
write a new gospel
according to Charles
BC, BL
1994 *Anno Lari*
We shall open a new window
on chronology, plunge
Caesar and Columbus
into a millennium of eclipse
Lara! Lara!
Papa Lara!
innocent babies babbling
'our father' tongues caught
in a slip, they cut their teeth
on Brian Lara's name
Lara! Lara!
Lara! Lara!
the almanac farmers swear by
outdating Sobers and McDonald
Men struggle with his strokes
both fore and after play
dance forward or move backward
graft, prod or put the sickle in

Women too pad up to read Lara
fake their horoscopes
to fall within his orbit
they learn new strokes in middle life
taking their chance 500 to 1
of becoming Lara's wife
       Lara! Lara!
       Lara! Lara!

NOT EXACTLY CRICKET

Nelson Mandela come to the crease
too late, too late
to build a hero's innings
I wonder why the Captain
send him in so late
If he doesn't get a chance
they must promote him in the order
next time round

So do God bless you
Mr. Speaker
Don't rule him out
of order too soon
Give the bowler onus of proof
and give him benefit of doubt
He must make the next century
and take our land
out of white people mouth.

FOR MANDELA

I cannot light a bonfire
in this British corridor
for you Mandela
It is the dry season
and men and trees are boors
Flames cannot dance
under a water curfew
and the fear of common law

But there is no bar
on Robben Island and Soweto
for you Mandela
Fires laugh freely in the kraals
night joins hand with day
to flame your colours in the sky
and you purchased rains from heaven
to season centuries of drought

I will light a bonfire
with my pen. A barrel of pride
for you Mandela
Paint your knowing smile
like a fragrant fire
for greener trees in a new morning
lighting blacks in all the world.

JIM ALLEN

Jim Allen is not out
the scores he wrote in black
and white at Hyde and Sturge Park
are still extant. Men tout
and sing his hits in chorus
whenever bat and ball cause
music to resound beyond the boundary

His nearly nervous shuffle
half-stoop, photographing
of the battle line were preludes
to a savage skirmish to rescue
his small island from oblivion
Women's dresses danced above their heads
exposing their appreciation for his deeds

One day in England he forgot
himself, whipped a white man's
ball in six successive sallies
and sent men scurrying to a distant field
like slaves. Jim was Glossop's master

He kept wicket too
tight like a secret
crouching low behind a wall
of sticks, he caught his man
red-handed if he nicked the ball
his hand held high with glee
demanded of the umpire *how is he?*

Jim could toss up his hand usefully
so pavilion pundits say
this time the media got it right
He snatched four lives in a pitched

fight at Hyde and sealed his hat trick
of devices to put the bulldog out.

Jim is not out
who pulled off feats
on tall fields black and white
he does not need my ball-
point bat to score his life-run
The turfs at Hyde and Sturge Park
are green with memories for centuries
His innings is not over.

SHORT OF A CENTURY

(For George Allen, island player, died 1990)

After hitting out at Hugo's
lightning pace your innings ended
with a short-pitched ball
ten before the century closed

You gave us oohs and aahs of ecstasy
and pain when you missed five score
by inches. The umpire's lean finger
checked the reign of runs

And gave you out. Your sun stood still
and shouted cheat at destiny
for breach of morning promise
a well-run field of gold

All-round player you stringed
your Wisden willow for guitar
and scored harmonies to thrill pavilions
at Bourda, Kensington and Cuba

Boos for the umpire over, I hear voices
glory day now de morning come
crowds are standing all over the pavilion
sing and shout now de morning come

My pen a primitive bat turned
upside down enters the chorus
to score a silent interlude
of hope and sorrow till morning come.

DEATH OF A FRIEND

(parson politician teacher cricketer)

They say you were a little hasty
your balls were quickies as they hurried
off the wicket as you 'came through',
Teacher George; but you also bowled
the moderate stuff. Thought you'd use them
when playing for the Pearly Gates.
You didn't stay for trifle (there is dessert
in heaven but that's not what I mean)
like waiting for a friend's return
to watch your innings close and celebrate
your trophies, man of the match and moment.

You were not too nice with protocol
so towels of lamentation
will do your memory wrong. Rather a conch shell
a peal of hands and a standing ovation
as you enter the pavilion to pad up
for a higher order of service.

Death did not intimidate you
but its quick delivery left us reeling
with a body blow. You went for 67,
short of a life-run, but you cheated time
of a prolonged match with sickness
and a slow crossing. We have no substitute
for you. Your team well-knit by blood
and brotherhood must limp along without you
but we will join you on a golder field
not Lord's but at Elysium where there is no appeal.

BARBADOS MEDLEY

The loaded donkey's clip-clop
never stopped
and on the greens
the players shouted:
how's that?

A man was out
another at the altar
the players and the bride
costumed in white
the mourners robed
in black and grey lent colour
to the pallid carnival
black-and-white give state
and dignity to death

Bone of my dust
and dust of my flesh
till death do us part
the parson chained them
with a knot of words
they drained the sacrament
foretaste of the purple fruits of life

The funeral hit the road
the wedding train gave chase
a double derby into sunset
the players on the green
appealed for light
the umpire stood
as silent as a stone

Brakes screech
horns scream
mourning tempers blaze
the wedding streamers
deck the hearse
whoa donkey! stop the car my love
let me hop off here
and skirt the traffic jam

The donkey's feet said clip clip clop
His regal rider muttered:
How's that?

COLUMBUS POEM

Dawns 1992 a magic landfall
on a brand new world of gold
in Europe. Columbus makes a second
coming after five hundred years
not to violate virgin peoples
but to carnival God for conquests
and their half-caste issues
nuggets for the church of Spain

And there shall be no more wars
and racial prejudice
Tate and Winban Cain and Lyle
shall lie together
like babies milking at one breast
children of bondsmaid rattle glasses
and tabor praises with the free
Arabia shall see the glory
great of Europe not the greed
Let Saddam Hussein hear and heed

And please, Chris, Montserrat not ready
for your second coming
Hugo took the place by storm the other year
stripping all our cover bare

Yes the town blazing loud with music
and we can't hear prophet Hammie preach
we putting back on our concrete
garments, but we still naked on a beach

After five hundred years Columbus coming
without sin unto celebration
and Europe, learning solidarity,
closes envious eyes to undivided property
And Chris(t), in Europe locked in unity
Whose colony shall Caribbea be?

ULTIMATE

'And the sea gave up the dead...
and they were judged' (*Revelation*, 20:13)

It is false
the sea will not give up
its honoured dead
the transit slaves
who dived into its deep
to rescue freedom.

Their bones are pearls
to gem the crown of Neptune
their bodies make a living sacrament
their spirits light eternal flames
for them there is no judgement.

The sea is sick
to vomit merchant men
who traded chains
those prisoners were martyrs
love-slaves of liberty
they have no case to answer
to die for freedom
is the ultimate morality.

HOLOCAUST

At the holocaust museum
in the heart of Washington
big men attired in ties
recited skeleton
facts like nursery rhymes
It was an object lesson
pictures worth a thousand groans
the pain of hate the penalty
of being convicted nobody
by somebody even if you are white.

I was not indifferent to their plight
black as I am my blood was red
when last I saw it
Who could be callous to naked
bubbies dancing in a death orgy
and the succulent waste of love?

Why therefore blame my pen
to mine tears from the fossils
of my race, open fissures
in the walls of history,
to itemize and audit scars?
No, I will follow destiny,
book keeper for the living and the dead.

There is no museum to slavery
in the head of London
or the heart of Washington

PRIVATE
(UK September 1991)

Privacy, an ironclad English quality
is patent on this railway platform
every morning. In clock-tight monotony
each one takes a stand in cold isolation
behind a paper curtain, a tobacco screen.
Lips zippered, none pollutes the heavy atmosphere
with carbon dioxide, only smoke.
In the face of a conservative recession
liberal twaddle about the weather
has lost currency. Silence is sterling.

This girl with ginger steps stands here
well-groomed besides the garbage bin
one foot slightly forward
to hold her balance behind *The Mirror*.
Hobble-skirted, this one painted like a star
makes an entry at five past eight
just three minutes to ogle openly
if you are not English. She melts into the set.
This coloured Briton listens silently like God
ears plugged, not generous like a genuine
West Indian playing sweet music
loudly humming let there be or deadening despair.

The train breaks the still picture.
It is born again within its moving womb
breathing room only, no place for speech
except you are West Indian.
Communion stops at Marks and Spencer's
bottoms, C & A tops.

Let Berlin break her wall
apartheid embarrassed, blush, backslide
Let Poland peddle new brand solidarity
England will be England
united at war and the Commonwealth games.

ROYAL GARDEN PARTY

Trust me to stay grounded
and not rise to the occasion
on my first visit to Buckingham Palace

grounds. Whites like red ants
enough to fill a colony
men in sartorial wonder. Top notch hats

like broad-brimmed chamber pots
morning dress in a dying afternoon
with tails like an undertaker's

guests clothed in knowledge of protocol
a sense of the occasion on their sleeves
though this woman's painted lips

had a brush with chocolate cake. Lizzie
looks so natural today
her make-up, made to measure, fits

How gross not to indite majestic flights
in rhymed heroic measure
after an intercourse with Charles

still heir, apparantly. Or some irony
of empire, a tenor windy
with patriotism like *Rule Britannia*

could have made me sing. My black lead
played instead below the belt
for instance where would people pee

in an emergency? There was no 'toilet
this way' sign, no outhouse looking
like a privy on this conservative

party plan. You couldn't hose
the royal grass and dampen protocol
or do you back the stage

and spout into the silent lake
careful not to make ripples
while the bandsmen finger their own

instruments to make more discreet music?
Trust me to be buried
in thoughts of such banality

like where to number one or two
in a natural emergency
in Buckingham Palace grounds.

MUGGED
July 31, 1995

Dogs are darlings to the English
If you are male and black
You can be mugged
With vicious allegations
If old, you are just a retired
Mugger on the dole
Beware the big stick on the beat
You can easily eat mess
On this dog shit English street

FOR KING AND COLONY

i

Presidents go
administrators come
commissioners go
governors come
changing white boots
like Buckingham Palace guards
we beat the same imperial drum
with carrot and stick
a monotonous hum
stuck
with the same stereo
types. Music softer
message dumb

Letters patent brown like autumn trees
but the leaves don't fall
it's the selfsame call
to divide the home circle
with ruler
and accomplices only

But the circle is broken
with zombies and masqueraders
dancing out of line
to the heavy bass strains
of Britannia rule the waves
and baa baa black sheep
have you any news
yes yes Majesty but no views
I have the head of John
the Boatist on a confidential file
a loyal royal Tom
I have peeped the extra mile

Civilised servants sit
at the rim of the circle
with dumb intelligence
and an Oxford smile
trading their kind
in an obtuse triangle
Blackburne to the White House
at Westminster
Same monotonous drumbeat
same fetters extant
same letters patent
from King Charles of blessed memory
same imperial authority
to divide and rule
this said island
'possessed by savage and heathern people'
with ruler and accomplices

ii

The points of the sceptre
are digging at my brain
when your bowels horn you
keener is the pain
My eyes were closed
but not in sleep
they are open to a vision
in a garden where I weep

iii

But a blotting old tears from mi eyes
ah goin turn de table
like a skilful Turner
we stop playing the fool
we goin play the song of freedom
play it cool real cool.

TOASTED MAJESTY

So nice that some things never change
like toasting healthy majesty
with drums and masquerade fatigue
from June to June under an English heaven.
The sovereign ages like good wine
the roses in her face are fadeless. She wears
well, it is hard to guess her years.
If anyone speaks ill of royalty
(Diana and Charles apart, *apparently*)
she turns both cheeks in absent
beauty and inherited grace.

So nice that some things never change
such as the monarch on parade.
Defence Force trumpets blare
the selfsame sound from year to year
with an occasional quaver.
The knapsack of problems in the economy
strikes a heavy note but on nobody's back
People are loyal; the soldiers stand
at ease still with nothing to defend
It is fun to fire the *feu de joie*
their guns' high point
And the children would scream
The children would scream

So nice that some things never change
empire children on display, a school of troops
drilled to make an English holiday
for generations of auspicious Junes
They are loyal though Churchill's voice
no longer thunders righteous war
from school walls cold and dull
and buns and muscovado kool-aid cease

(Caribbean canes are bad for health today
and Europe sugars John Bull's tea)
but guns ring out a roll of honour
for the Queen and the children scream
The children would scream

So nice that some things never change
the Governor's plumed head, our pillow
of security his crown white-liveried
laundered innocent like the hands of Pilate.
Native soldiers present arms
a little out of step with new technology
but Britons *never shall be slaves*
while our mock army drills to fire
the *feu de joie*, with precision
their guns' high point
And the children would scream
The children would scream.

So nice that some things never change
buntings stream no more, wind and water
in recession. Younger (not Kipling's lesser) breeds
never hipped on royalty neglect to wave
the union jack, more tolerant of spades
tropic clouds no longer echo hip hurray
leaving majesty a little short of sunshine
but soldiers strict to rule lend three cheers
and coolly fire the *feu de joie* at gun point
But the children would scream
The children would scream.

So nice that some things never change
the odd cynic, hair straight as cane leaves
ungrateful for emancipation and the gift of tongue
stigmatises the Queen's rep, pedigree
and pigment to affirm bad talk and blackness
but well know in their permed hearts

better he than johnny late from long shirt village.
With her man in the capital, the Queen's largesse
is safe. So let the guns fire the *feu de joie*
Though the children would scream
The children would scream.

So nice that some things never change
the smart of soldiers on parade
on Remembrance Day, the white-washed cenotaph
at the city centre, an obelisk to the folly
of war. Its clock like a giant eye
transplanted from Big Ben to watch
this museum copy of our history
ticking off our dead who fought to keep our mother
free for Europe's penetration
Rich in sterling patriotism our soldiers
do not devalue the *feu de joie*
And the children would scream
The children would scream.

So nice that some things never change
in this fiefdom of exotica
Cattle carts like disabled veterans
pressed out of service but unarmoured cars
of uppity blacks ring charade square
not red nor white just clichéd lush-green
Domestic trumpets bray new emerald airs
but bars of bonnie braes still fret the song
Times are hard but the masses will not starve
for ceremony and circus while guns
ring out the *feu de joie*
And the children can scream
The children can scream.

So nice that some things never change
Britannia rules but makes no waves
and we prise development alms annually

from the palms of Dover and a hard face
to keep us "as the Caribbean used to be"
We still pay tribute not in cotton bales
but canonical courtesies to the English
charge hand. No sweat, we no longer climb
sugar chimneys or coconut trees
to cool the master's thirst
and they dress us in the MBE at close of play
while the guns still echo the *feu de joie*
And the children would scream
The children would scream.

So nice if some things never change
and not corrupt like politicians waxing stale
in office hoarding power to resist
the scrap of history, embalmment
for the archives, the mess of worms
and clinical dig of goggled *ologists*
Long live St. George's Hill its rusted plaque
blazoning it a collector's item
a tourist piece with currency from the Queen's
howitzers pointed at native guards
who bark the *feu de joie*
Though the children scream
The children would scream.

So nice that some things never change
babies graduate from home-made *hippin*
to khaki diapers and army fatigues
from overseas. They pack kitbags
of the national state for another's back
and smile, train guns to stutter
birthday honours for the Queen,
their lives' high point
But children still scream
The children still scream.

BEHIND GOD BACK

You come from a two-be-three island
hard like rock
black you have another handicap
and you come from Long Ground
way behind God back.

They taught you like a fool
never told you miles of cotton
went to Liverpool
to line the Bank of England
from Long Ground behind God back
he shoulda turned round
and catch the thieves white-handed
white and black

They took you for an imbecile
never told you Montserrat tobacco
made W.D. and H.O. Wills
rich testators of Bristol University
lighting their names on the crest of history
with Long Ground tobacco
bought behind God back

Never told you how your mother strong
to carry buckra cotton
and his seed
fertile like Long Ground soil
strong to carry bales of history
and buckra deeds heavy like a sack
of cotton picked behind God back

People in the town
didn't know off-white and brown were black
until they went to England
Powell vote to pack them back
rejected like stained cotton
didn't know when God turned round
his smile like a rainbow
lit Long Ground with hope
and cotton children weave boot strap
to pull themselves up
from behind God back

IMPORTED SPEECH

West Indian abc and simile
are copyright in London
like slaves and letters patent
tongues come in ships
as white as snow
like Mary's learned lamb
they stick to you like burrs

Factors did not know the abc
of sugar apple sweet as cane
they spread false humour
natives lolling under palms
in sun and rain
not a chink of truth
in a nutshell p for palm
hard water making kernel
white as milk
eluded English merchants

Standing under breadfruit shade
we counted loss in acorn cups
e for elephant easier to swallow
than a garden lizard's egg
blind to calypso colours
poinciana petals
rioting in a tropic wind
we coldly swayed with daffodils

Our fathers were figures
of speech Master Willy Mr. Dan
grist fodder fuel
ciphers in a golden plan
pyramids built with brazen hands

Now we have a head condition
an imported spirit
drunken to the lees
taste for ads and alien apples
frozen qs and peas.

INSTEAD OF SNOW

They say we're lucky without snow
At Christmas, just a warm poinsettia glow

Buntings of hibiscus ablaze
With glory shepherding praise

To God o'er cush-cush hills of yam
No Herodian terrorists to alarm

The sheep and fondle virgin boys
And guns are harmless television toys

That shatter shadows' bloody screen.
We imagine what reality might have been

They say we do not miss the mistletoe
in Montserrat, the coconut will do

For kissing; a trellised moon upon your head
But beware the fruit, a stone instead

Sorrel blood is just as red as holly berry
And pomegranates and clammy cherry

Make good Christmas trees; their fruits like lights
From mini moons bewitch the night

Instead of snow we'll export masquerade
Patented with a Montserratian trade

Mark. Native colours kept intact
Music cut in a lively country tract

For them great folly to emigrate
From such a simply rich estate

They say we're lucky to live in Montserrat
But wouldn't want to change their lot

Of money burdening wintry trees
They love their milky north more than West Indies.

VIRGIN GORDA
1993

I slept on virgin Gorda
a full night under blue canopy
white sheets and did not breach
her privacy I found her man
grove inlet delicious undergrowth
combed coves and promontories
to soft music from the lapping of the sea
savoured her brackish waters
but did not silt her gully beds
break the seal or bypass security

I found in my hedonic age
an ancient clay pot of respect
for sacred things in spite of me
my symbols harden as I write
imagining what pleasures might have been
had I given libido full throttle
No mean achievement I did not pollute
the virgin Gorda or my verse
controlled instead my personal irony
and struck a note for fantasy

I wonder what mischief you get up to
with those infant virgins in your ken
a fallen Jerusalem hard by
in a moon when paedophilia
is no more a Cardinal sin
but lines and imagination must,
like lust, be metered, kept in check
so that burdened priests and poets
can maintain their heads erect

I took no topless brochures
exposures of your secret parts, lest some Drake,
Attila, philistine sailor man
less circumspect, rush there to strip
your beauty, violate your bath
and swear that you seduced him
I left your feet swept clean
your grail still holy and alone.

CARIBBEAN UNITY

A new wave is breaking, breaking
with a flourish on Caribbean sands
cresting boldly like Columbus' caravels
with cargoes of sorrow,
is breaking in Demerara
choking the shouts of Kaietur
muddying the message of rivers
silting the dreams of sucklings,
is breaking on the Bocas in Trinidad
mugging the hum of birds
drowning harmony with a melancholy roar,
is breaking, lashing white skirts
at Bathsheba like a masochist
hijacking fishes in flight across Barbados,
is breaking in St. Thomas
lapping at the portal of the virgin
islands penetrating their hinterlands
without a green card or health certificate
depositing loess from America,
is breaking on a medium wave
band in islands called saints
filling their dishes with exotic pot-
age in exchange for their birthright
in prime time

A crime wave is breaking, breaking
in Jamaica like the bark of guns
in overcast skies farting shame
in the face of the sun,
is breaking, breaking with getaway speed
washing up weed all over land,

is breaking at Birds Internecine Airport
in Antigua where sun and sewer
do not smell beauty any more

And Montserrat ever swimming against
the fickle tides of Caribbean Unity
is beginning to break

They are praying for recession.

LAMENT FOR MAURICE BISHOP

Bishop
high priest of Grenada
land of spice
and putrid sacrifice
why so sudden flight
in undressed wounds
standby for paradise

Blood clots on the sceptre
sully the bright sword
forged in revolution fires
your blood
your father's blood twice dead
the people's blood heavy
like a guillotine on your head

What evensong you sang
at Mount Moritz or Moriah
did you chant
Das Kapital or King James
did you breathe the names
of Marx and angels
was Fidel faithful to your call
helpless hero
before the lamentable fall

They say ghosts march past in silence
at Fort Rupert
sire's sepulchre
son's doomed altar
revolution's wasted rampart
Grenada's Golgatha

Will you come back to meditate your land
do armies muster where you are
do men still aspire
do sudden storm clouds tumble down
shipwrecking high desire

Bishop of Grenada
land of spice
were you embalmed
checked out so soon for paradise

INFORMAL

This man couldn write
a straight line
but he mowed blades of cane
in perfect rhyme
couldn read
the time in a clock's white face
he dialled the sun
at any moment in the day
and told its riding pace
divined the watch of night
by the tenor of an ass's bray
couldn count
on the stock exchange
hum to the fickle rhythm
of the market
he valued livestock
at a glance
'praised damage at the prance
of his neighbour's hoofs
this man had no bachelor certificate
but he didn marry
work-and-study at a free academy
slept where he ate.

DAMNICK

You see dat man in de han-
Me-down pants. His name is Damnick

He never darken de door of a school
But words in his mouth like hot pepper

Seeds. Damnick ehn no fool

Sense in his head to tickle de bones
Of de dead and puncture de pride

Of cloud-hatted philosophers
And make learning look like a clown

Damnick teeth white like a light
Devouring de dark. Words run through

His lips like silver veins in de belly
Of the earth and rhythm in a dead

Goat skin. Nough sense in his head

Damnick is deaf-mute to metaphor
Bat-blind to imagery but he is always harping

Life is an orchestra with bossy directors
Who want cat and daag to jitter-

Bug to deh tune. But he ehn no fool

No han-me-down fiddle and no second base
He gonna honk his own horn

Damnick know his place. No cracked quavers for he
Or blue minor key. In his poor-great country

All Damnicks are in the majority

If he can't get a trumpet to blow
His own mind as loud as he choose

He will ping no man's pong on no empty
Oil pan. He will break up the wand

Or blow his own fuse. Damnick ehn no fool.

TIMO

To see Timo lying there on hospital
bed in a pale garment as unfashionable
as a shroud to cover his privates
is quite disturbing, if you knew
Timo when he was Timo
He would chop his hoe in the belly
of the soil and make stones ring with pain
finish a task at Tar River mountain
before the sun opened his eyes good
on the world. Used to clap loud loud
in church and wind up his waist
to give you and the Lord laugh
and the Lord would laugh

Timo could cut down a mountain
of ground food and mop his bowl
and his teeth with his tongue clean clean
You should see Timo laugh
like he goin dead: he bends at the waist
hands on his head, bellow deep
from his belly in sharps and flats
Timo has king-size feet
Cassia barely see them coming and begins
to cry. Now a whole foot is helpless
can't even mash a fly

Timo just lying there on hospital
cot like a child not a word
beyond his breath, chest barely heaving
mouth blowing bubbles to burst
in an instant. A dumpling can bite him
and he don't know

He can hardly shoo away death
from his own backyard like a fowl
or tell him a big bad-word

What is man eh boy, what is man eh?

BACK THEN THE HORSE

1

Back then the horse, mahogany brown to black,
was the cadillac of travel
(whites also ruled the road in the minority).
Feet shod with fire it tap-danced
to its own music, cobbled feet beat on street
clocking-up clocking-up wide-nosed mile.
Linking hinterland to town it doubled up
messenger-express and luxury line.
Designed for speed horses changed
a range of gears; sometimes a dancing steed
with a pirouette and a reel in horsepower show
a reel and a pirouette just for so;
sometimes a cruise tourist pace
while green beauty bathed its face
and then a change to a galloping gait
ambling ambulance four-wheel drive
steep chase to a long-distant doctor.
When physic failed, the horse
hied home bringing the death
certificate, a decent haste to arrest
decay, the rising smell of hell
on earth, or heaven on rare occasions.
No tap-dance then, a pensive dirge
in measured beat, long feet on street.

2

Asses trotted in another class
by no means in the rear
they could easily pass as a beat-up van
for fractious rides at a cheaper fare.

Built for freight they were forced
to accommodate a chauffeur and riding mate.
If carefully greened and broken-in well
it sometimes came to pass
the master rode to town upon a virgin ass.
I wonder how they earned the honour
of stupidity, for I've seen them upset
a noble horse in an asinine derby.
Back then a shortage of chronometers
obliged us to tell the time of day
by a loud alarm a jack ass's bray

3

On God's travel menu a la carte
instead of a BMW ride to heaven
I'll punch a horse or donkey cart.

AT GRAMMAR SCHOOL

That it was a grammar school
was absolutely patent, trade marked
in Harrow. The ablative absolute
like British rule a little hard to swallow.
At Long Ground men kept *keepers*
but *puellam amavero* was gibberish
they don't know nothing so.
Fluent in creole, parroting
and paraphrasing Shakespeare hurt
your mother's tongue and you mouthed Moliere
without the accent. Caesar's Gallic
wars put you at risk for colic
an acute accusative of indigestion

The school was a private ward
for top notch boys with double digit egos.
But what counted was their pocket
book and high estate, cultivated
by the man in street their senior, *billy*
bound to call them Master to their face

A foolhardy few of us arrived
past the common entrance
togaed in green and orange ties for greatness.
Full black, you were handicapped
by the illogic of a metaphysics
which made it right for pot
to label kettle black at grammar school.
The problem wasn't purely colour, it was pig
mentation pseudo-pedigree and class-
ic illiteracy at grammar school

We learned to use Prospero's tongue
rewrote the narrow tract,
posted pickets of verse, and blocked
the gate with lancet words,
opened up a broad highway, a common
entrance for the child in the street
unravelling the arcane plot of the elite.

GRADUATION FEVER

There is a sudden rash
of going down ceremonies
spreading like measles
a smart brain wave
to spark a dull economy
babies leap-frog from breasts
to bigger things ahead of years

Tenderhearted kindergartens
do-it-yourself gerontologists
borderlining dote age
(some on trial) pass out
with distinction dressed in state

Seamless gowns of knowledge
trademarked in the USA
topped with British caps belled
with tassels from Taiwan a meld of culture
cover a multitude of sins
like the skirts of acolytes and parsons

Brown leaves from a closed chapter
turn over spelling errors miscalculations
wrong dates and *bad words* signed
and sealed with a certificate
celebrated by the lady with a harp
One gown fits all

This academic epidemic
is healthy for small island ego
its threat to come-of-age ripens
every summer. Our motherland
should give us full credit
put us on the Queen's list
for a decent bursary or burial

This is the day of the diploma
and personal computer pirate print
unsure like paper kerchiefs washed
in the local off-shore laundry
Hope some badjohn student does not wave
a counterfeit certificate in Peter's face
in an essay to pass the port to heaven
another way.

I trust this graduation epidemic
does not breed immunity
to education regarding it as academic
like children who often whipped
to Sunday school with threat of prayer
and candle become insensitive
to service and shut the message out.

WHEN JUSTICE CAME TO CHURCH

Justice came to church on Monday
in rank order on *me* Lord's day
robed in solemn splendour
black-skirted caps off white

The learned judge did not throw
the book of the law at any
in particular just a loaded lesson
bowing at the Lord's name in due process

The message from the cloth was pre-
meditated but no crime. The law
was put on trial for mugging
mercy, no bail for the innocent

The rector made no altar call
And none came to the bar unbidden
A man of great faith he hoped the lawyers
Settle out of court with heaven

The service being professional
it could not be fully on the house
of God. Just a free-will offering,
recessional drinks were on the judge

Absent from the body, prisoners
said amen in spirit. On caution
justice left the Lord's court
in rank order just as it came in

I hope his Lordship does not indict me
for contempt. I will plead innocence
and retain a Queen's big wig to cite
poetic freedom, my licence to indite.

TAMARIND TREE AT ST. ANTHONY'S

Centenarian guard
You keep immortal vigil like a saint
With a grave forehead in a grey churchyard

The wind blows
A solemn descant of sorrow
in your branches. Touched by our woes

Your brown leaves fall
Carelessly silent like tears
A weary corpus christi of mortal

Dolour furrows your face
Fat priests prey on pious people
Peddling magic like God's grace

Carib kills Arawak
For altar girls and shamans
Whites dressed in Indian weed attack

Blacks with a cat-o-nine cross
Cut from your limbs on pain of mutilation
Making you a complice and comrade in loss

You raised green buntings
Scattered confetti in the whirlwind of freedom
Until creole oppression opened new fountains

Centenarian guard
Condemned to witness restless wrongs
Without parole or sleep in the silent barracks yard.

EASTER

This April is so hot. Hungry
for mischief the devil is cooking
a pot of hurricanes prematurely
to obeah this green island.

Baked by the lenten sun
earth seems dead, nothing to feast
your eyes. A resurrection
is wished by the devout.

But three iguanas find a green leaf
high on a tree of thorns
and I can see life returning
to the garden and the distant

Scent of lilies. No need to kill iguanas
or Barabbas anymore
his son may bind the winds
and bruise the head of hurricanes.

DON'T BLAME GOD

It is a sin to label God
indelicate to dress our parents
in a garden without covering,
a mere chiffon of flowers. The climate

User-friendly not hot or cold
only passion's heat, bottoms could be bare
it was no treat to wear a tan
their ready-made suit already black

Man's eyes were not yet open
to the underbelly of beauty
God's super x-ray vision shot past
modesty and imagination to nakedness

No need to cover their hair
for service in the open air
Besides, who has a feel for breasts
but babies? Cain's seed still in the tomb

Before man intercoursed with words
and conceived corruption, no need
to cover up. God sentenced him:
"Be born again" and swaddled him in skin

We have graduated since to briefs
transparencies and bottomless attire
so God will finally have his way
when we return stripped for service naked

It is a sin to label God indecent
to dress us naked, shifting blame
He paved a broad way to our desires
to manufacture shame.

GRAVE BEAUTY

Our village famous for its rhizome
furrows tous-les-mois tannias arrowroot
none like my mother's dusty home

For beauty purple bougainvillaea sweet lime
red exoria myrtle scenting evergreen love
flowers cut down in their prime

To dye the face of death
ultimate metaphor fit for God
sad beauty tombing mortal breath

Our village beautiful for rhizome
furrows mounds of mercy for the poor
none like my mother's flower-cold home.

YOU WAS A FREEDOM FIGHTER, MA

You was a freedom fighter, Ma
when you pout yuh mout'
pon estate man
tekking liberty wid yuh sun-tanned skirt
just because yuh house a grow pon e lan'
not because you nuh train gun
ina World War One
you is a freedom fighter, Ma.

When you knead flour and water
into hard leaven bread
patch pappie pants wid needle and thread
to keep wind and neaga mout'
out of his battie
when yuh ban' yuh belly
for the long-term good of yuh six picknee
like IMF battening down de poor
in a mawga economy
you is a freedom fighter, Ma

When you vote 'gainst white helmet in 1951
withdrew yuh blood from estate corn
robbing it of love and fertility
cut you eye pon de cotton
black boll dem dung
though de buckra man
wok you down to de groun'
you is a warrior, Ma

When heavy wid toil
you fell asleep on one knee
kissing God foot
to set you six picknee free
He didn't have to make dem

Permanent Secretary
as long as dey pick bread in dignity
you didn' want dem to be no man's lackey
you just wanted dem out of slavery
so dey could sing and write
their own imagery
paint a fresh canvas in history
you is a freedom fighter, Ma

Though no one knows
where yuh grave door turns
and you're not even numbered
among the unknown
you is a freedom fighter, Ma.

BEETLE
(7.7.94)

In direct flight from some uncharted space
it crash-landed on my bed
A stab of fear arrested
my attention from the O.J. Simpson show
plotting his escape by television
with smart accomplices and a gun

The beetle had no murder weapon
yet in revenge I plopped him in the toilet
sink. It landed like a life boat
upside down, pushed out mysterious oars
and paddled the entire sluice
in search of life

For this beetle smart enough
to break the law of aerodynamics
float, fly and crawl in the same gear
insanity was not a plausible defence
he was more than just a hum bug
Yet for some uncharted reason
I bailed him out leaving O.J. in suspense.

PREJUDICE

This resourceful Montserratan was murdered
In the same time zone as O.J. Simpson's wife
But in a prouder moment. She was smitten
In her own saloon pleading at the bar of life

Her presumed assailant was not a star
Just a smoking fire stick, yet a job expertly done
Like surgery, but he received no footage
On the screen, no palms were won

Underexposed her image remained dark
Her worth eclipsed. Pity she did not attract
Some cur of high degree, a king of coke
Smutty calypsonian or a minister sacked

For larceny. Hard to catch the camera's eye
Even in crime if you a low, a Mr. Who?
Another prisoner. Hope heaven is not reserved
For elite crooks; underdogs need glory too.

LOVE BIRDS

Flying late to work
two black birds on a naked bough
arrested my attention.
Spitting in each other's mouth
they made a show of love
at high noon on the broadway.
I wonder do they ever quarrel
under cover over bill
of rights, call each other names
in sharp avian tongue
make swords from their beaks
differ violently on who should lead
the colony when recession peaks?
Do hen-pecked cases of battered cocks
appear in feathered court?
Do they behave like some reptiles
showing their true colour
when light fades as we frail humans do?

I bet they came out here
to scribble a mock metaphor
stage a scene
and carp at human beings
who call each other love birds.

LOVE'S ECONOMY
(For a friend)

You oppress me
with your heavy toll
    of friendship

You dispense munificence
with artful hand
    in unmetred measures

like cruel punishment
by a distempered parent
    illiterate in love's administration

Your dollops of investment
on my love's stock
    exchange cloy me

It is legitimate to give and get
but my love prefers to barter
    in a slimmer market

with stakes within my reach
Self-love like an insane terrier
    is better kept on leash.

WIFE POEM
(February 14, 1993)

You are my inlet. After the day's row
I harbour safely from life's undertow
Your gentle eddies bathe my salted feet
Like balm, and settled in your warm retreat

I dream new labours on wanton water
Though toils and tossing do not matter
In my ricochet from the wheel and rack
Love's hinterland ministers to my lack

New odysseys pull me like a poem
And a stern voice warns me of my solemn
Covenant with despotic duty
But your bosom is a lodestar guiding me

You are my inlet. After the long row
I nestle warmly from life's undertow.

THIRD BIRTHDAY

(For Coretta)

From the third arc of time
You walk from toddling innocence
With firmer tread the circle of the years

The sun smiles on your hope
You laugh like nature's music
May friendly stars rule your brittle run

The fourth watch hurries on
The eleventh impatient waits
Adorn the years with evergreen leaves of learning

Stride on with gifts of hate and love
Assaulting wrong with hateful brow
Loving hallowed freedom with maturing blood

PUBERTY

To have puberty creep upon your daughter
like a secret is as much a shock
to you as it is to her, a haemorrhage
in a healthy mind, a maiden tremor
on a quiet lake triggering a vein of fear
nature's sick idea of a practical joke

Without splitting hairs (stuffed bosoms apart)
there should be warning signs
like blood-shot eyes, off-colour fingernails
schools of birds swimming in the skies
like an omen. When hogs dance it will rain
and moons can tell tomorrow's weather

Your daughter needs to pad up for her opening
period at the wicket like a prudent bat
balls can surprise you in this sticky
atmosphere. She should have a rite
to celebrate the run of innocence
and the new pubic dispensation

(Stuffed bosoms apart) I hope the next stage
comes with ceremony, exchange of ribs
and a dance licence. To have puberty trickle down
your daughter like a secret is no romance
as much a shock to parent as to child
both can have a heart attack.

EARLY MORNING EXERCISE

Amusing vistas greet your eyes
At early morning exercise

Parked all night on an unlawful pasture
a car jogs home in the sly light
of a late moon dressed in a sari
of cloud, caught out by day

Slick shepherds teach their sheep
to climb their neighbour's fence
some other way and crudely prune
her bougainvillaea with poisoned teeth
Cowboys with a feel for paps cheat
infants of their mother's milk

Cattle egrets migrate to fish
for worms in new mown waves
far beyond their colony
teaching government how to stem the flight
of capital with a mixed economy

Meddling in the dark with new technology
grandfather frogs spill their meat
fresh as the dew in a headlamp
collision. You can feast your eyes
before the prying sun pollutes
and a festival of flies

An industrious boat busy while customs sleep
drops its cargo in a silent bay
before the drunken waves wake and break
the news in manifest morning light
At this chaste hour city streets
are sober flushed by sleep

beggars like preachers are at prayer
for blessings on their industry
oily tongues and a discriminating eye

Chances Mountain in a dark green mask
cables a mystery of mermaids
ponds and spirits; its dragon breath
of sulphur mocks mortality
dictating salvation with tongues of fire.

Dead secrets decorate the street
in haste, fallout from garbage bins,
no sense of taste. Private lives
pulled impiously this way and that
by prowling dogs, off scent

Amazing what you smell at peep
of morning if you are that way bent.

MEANING

This weather cock
perched on that sky tower
cannot read the signs of the time
to describe these searing moons as fine
with subterranean pots
boiling over with sizzling heat
and growing a tuber
like pulling teeth

It pours and birds
basking under grey cloud cover
genuflect a praise
fruits put new colour in their cheeks
ghauts flush with pride
gutters get a shower
but "it is a rotten day"
the garbled message from the tower

I hope their tongue
is more explicit in semaphore
directing traffic
lest a pilot hearing, "right"
(If I may speak darkly)
takes the wrong angle
and crashes over Bermuda
in an obtuse triangle.

REMEMBRANCE

(September 17, 1992)

On hurricane remembrance days
the Aztecs raised pyramids
of praise on bloody altars
with heartrending sacrifice
for their spared lives
They mollified gourmet gods
who diet on marinated boys

September 17 is Hugo anniversary
hibiscus poppies bloom on wasted corms
blood-red like Flanders Field
dressing a garland fit for the Queen
on Remembrance Day

But dark clouds sit on the war memorial
like birds of ill omen
God moves his chairs angrily
threatening an outburst
a tantrum of thunder
poppy wreaths do not appease
godly appetite trained on blood
flesh alone, meet for remission

Today is Hugo holiday
wind-shed on our history
hibiscus poppies smile
upon the waste, gladdening September
A rumour rolls among the clouds
ill-starred day, remember

HURRICANE ROMANCE

(September 17, 1993)

Time flies; born yesterday
boys sprout beards, girls see red
change contour and countenance
and Hugo anniversary is never far away
all in a hellish speed to judgement day
Heads grey at early morning
grappling with decision to invest
in sugar tablets or pay insurance bills
Which dollar will abort damnation
change the direction of the wind
stop the bailiff's feet
or regulate my racing heartbeat

Time flies; born yesterday
children are ripe today
and a hurricane romance is never far away.

IN HUGO MEMORIAM (1994)

In sacred memory of our beloved
Hugo born of a virgin
on a wet September night
his horror scope harboured
good winds; it was a shot
in the vein of a sick economy
inflating it to dizzy heavens
ensuring high prices and a speedy
recovery. Hugo rocked the island
with music and tongues of fire
echoed over many waters
calling nations like a revival
to Montserrat Beaulah land

We celebrate Hugo child of God
he killed and made alive for a season
men at prayer for a Christmas hurricane
are not entirely out of reason.

LUIS PASSED
9:12:95

From the rout of Antigua
Luis dropped by
to pay personal respects
to Volcano an ally

He landed in haste
in the van of September
we still have his autograph
marks to remember

He pinched up our roofs
made mats on mattresses
peed on the floor
wet dreams of distress

To patent his passing
he bared trees of their leaves
they wept in their branches
tears dripped from our eaves

Steps lit by lightning
Luis went on a loot
an eye for green mangoes
and Bligh's poor breadfruit

Onto Anguilla
his passion unspent
in supine surrender
she got the full strength

Of a multiple rape
Marilyn also came
the feminine brand
of naked mayhem

A visit to the Virgins
Uncle Sam's daughters
no collect of saints
could cancel the slaughter

So Luis passed
and harassed with impunity
covering injustice
with natural immunity.

BIBLE ON THE HILL
02:12:95

Dressed in flaming underwear
Soufriere opened a new bible
in her pulpit on the hills
to teach us the arithmetic of days
in symbols red like fire
The first exodus
was on an August day
Today is day two
of the second exodus
six whole days for the feast of fire
six for the fast of light
but the clouds lifted
on the seventh day
and behold another dome
rested on the mountain
after four months of toil
bringing the sum to three
an awful trinity

How many days I wonder
until domes-day
genesis
of the final examination and the con-
summation of all things
Will we pass
out
down
into the crater lake
or up
to God knows
where?

ECLIPSE
26.2.98

God's eye twinkled
at his handiwork
His voice elided like a slip
half-moon crescent sun
in a circle of eclipse
radiating spokes of cheer
to a paradise half undone
by mountain fireworks
another natural display gone wrong
for His mercies endureth for ever.
And blackness finally had its day
of glory in the heavens
inspite of what word spinners say
and metaphors that maim us.

There is a harshness in the word eclipse,
its yoke of consonants
like a bad *cut-eye*
a cutlass lash
sudden fall of an axe
on a tree full of sap
an avalanche of ash blanking
years of sun and harvest song in Montserrat.

God's own creatures were confused
by his dazzling handiwork
of beauty and blinding light,
like want of co-ordination in a ministry
or a people unprepared
for a planned emergency.

Bats went to work at the rise
of the wrong moon,
their rest disturbed
drumming on roofs off tune.
White egrets quit the field
before close of play; worms
in a tight economy stopped their pay;
the alarm of force-ripe cockerels
was untimely triggered
by an unschooled ass's bray
who misread a plantain slice of light
for fourteen carat day;
female fowls responded
to the unseasonal arousal
against their wiser inclination.

And the eclipse in Montserrat was total
followed by a flood of light
but it wasn't the end of the tunnel.
Soufriere still hangs dark curtains on the sky
for his mercies endureth for ever.

THE NEW WAVE
(Birmingham, December 1996)

queuing up for houses
they claim their father's built — E.A. Markham

Thanks to the ulcers of soufriere
and their erratic inflammations
we are in the capital at last,
we do not walk on gold but have tasted
streets on ice and the white Christmas
which we dreamed has become a grey reality
with a light drizzle of kindness.
We are now into research and well poised
to possess houses our fathers built, outhouses
added inside. With furniture cut to fit
and flesh-pink plates we queue up for designer
mouths to skin our teeth like England.
and shrug lamb's wool at winter. Impressions
are important here. This time round the crown
is in our corner, not to heist; let the rabble
heckle, we are no longer strangers
not even to the cuppa tea, only the spelling,
drilled as we are in phonics; loyal teachers
have already driven English into us by heart.
England can take some credit for our learning
and the unintended fall outs. There is redemption
for colonial bonds to our mutual interest.
Label us asylum seekers if the words
caress the cash, stereotypes can salve,
a tenement for exchange of stock or labour
is just as sweet as is sea island sugar;
the transaction tickles God. Good winds
have blown us here (it was fire really
and the ulcers of soufriere); they wrought relief
and kinder memories of Britannia
in advance. The Queen is worth the song and save
if she takes care, not to break the wave.

HEIGHTS

Afraid of heights I did not climb
tall trees though ripe fruits
teased me with their luscious cheeks
the highest palm was out of reach

I burned the soot-stained lamp
for second third perhaps fourth place
no appetite for jackpot prize
the private pinnacle is lonely

heights attract eyes brown green
eyes of admiration eyes of hate
hungry eyes shoot fire
that burn the brittle props of power

Coward I avoid the giddy eminence
the politic applause
lean hands that itch to hail
a friend's exalted fall

AT FIFTY-FIVE
(July 1993)

Not much to show at fifty-five
grateful to have survived
tedious tossings numerous rocks
from friendly foes without and in
here double ditches, there a grin

Not much to show
a few certificates on my wall
with faded names a hint of rust
and yellow knowledge ripe for dust
amo amas I loved and lost
and learnt that love is tears of things
tears, silver drops to wash gold rings

Not much to show
barely three kids a mere shadow
of my father's ample quiver
abstemious, not a staunch
teetotaller but a rounded life
witness the sculpture of my paunch

Not much to show
Crow's-feet dot my face like errors
in my essay, too many to delete
and my head white as harvest
will not brook a colour counterfeit

Not much to show at fifty-five
few poems escaped the editor's chaff
so not entirely written off
as a writer. I still soar and sing
though his red pen wounds my wing

Not much to show
a node of contradictions
fed by a fanatic faith in Christ
and strong convictions of a paradise
with choice and an alternate menu
free from the tyranny of milk and honey

Not much, not very much to see
But I am learning how to be

AGING

I assemble evidence of aging
unwittingly. This hundred dollar

bill in my hip pocket
outlived months of wear, tear

and sat upon, by reason of strength
It came out crushed and wrinkled

unlike Her Majesty's face
on paper, fresh and fadeless

(On paper money, I mean)
Its survival at my posterior

like a chronic ailment is a post
script, a forgotten note

on memory rich evidence of age
and the wrinkled face of death.

AT COVER

I made the inside cover of a Caribbean
anthology made in England, temperate mercy
from a bumper crop of tropic poets

but I cannot scan the consolation.
in cricket I would train the water cart
and pad up for the selectors' second

thoughts. But the gleaners did not salve
the swelling boomers who like Agrippa
almost made it. Our comfort teams with doubt.

Even if the makers make another flight
they did not pre-book my passage
some counter clerk may *bounce* me out

I cannot tarry for a second coming
(that should read edition) to score my piece
and reincarnation dies in the white heat of my creed

Heaven is nice, a languid evening sipping bouts
of milk and honey without horns but my heart
will not be fit to play or stomach poetry

There is no purgatory for poets
If I merit print set me in the deep
past cover before I am extinct.

THE GOLD WATCH

Decorated with a gold watch at dusk of day
A fellow sojourner had grey days of wonder

Will this watch recount golden days past
Or will it measure new nights of unrest?

It keeps a straight face but its incessant tick
is a relentless reminder that work should not cease

I woke on time clocked on time took time for tea
Now this golden gift will watch time waste me

And I must hear its mocking monotonous rhyme
Keeping watch with its dial I'll die dead on time.

NOTES

B.C. Lara p.11
Anno Lari, Latin for "in the year of Lara".

For King and Colony p. 29
Turner is a reference to a British Governor in Montserrat in 1989

Toasted Majesty p. 31
"Never shall be slaves" is a phrase from the song "Rule Britannia" sung by children of the British Empire.
Feu de joie: French for "fire of joy", referring to a gun volley in honour of the sovereign.
"The way the Caribbean used to be": an island catch-word to attract tourists.

Behind God Back p. 35
W.D. and H.O. Wills were wealthy tobacco merchants of Bristol, England.

Virgin Gorda p.41
Virgin Gorda is one of the British Virgin Islands; Fallen Jerusalem is another.
Cardinal is a reference to a US Roman Catholic Cardinal who was accused (apparently falsely) of carnally molesting a student priest.

Caribbean Unity p. 43
Bathsheba is on the rougher south-western coast of Barbados.

Tamarind Tree at St. Anthony's p. 60
Reference to a tamarind tree at the entrance of the historic St. Anthony's Anglican church in Montserrat. Slaves who took their master to church, not being allowed to enter the place of the holy, sat under it.

You is a Freedom Fighter, Ma p.63
1951, the year of the first election under universal adult suffrage in Montserrat.

Early Morning Exercise p. 62
Chances Mountain is the highest mountain in Montserrat; it craters a pond where, according to legend, a mermaid lives.

Remembrance p. 75
The Aztecs believed in human sacrifice. Hurricane Hugo, one of the worst of the century, devastated Montserrat, St. Croix and other Caribbean territories in September 17 to 18, 1994.

OTHER RECENT POETRY
FROM PEEPAL TREE

Geoffrey Philp

HURRICANE CENTER

El niño stirs clouds over the Pacific. Flashing tv screens urge a calm that no one believes. The police beat a slouched body, crumpled like a fist of kleenex. The news racks are crowded with stories of pestilence, war and rumours of war. The children, once sepia-faced cherubim, mutate to monsters that eat, eat, eat. You notice a change in your body's conversation with itself and in the garden the fire ants burrow into the flesh of the fruit.

Geoffrey Philp's poems stare into the dark heart of a world where hurricanes, both meteorological and metaphorical, threaten you to the last cell. But the sense of dread also reveals what is most precious in life, for the dark and the accidental are put within the larger context of season and human renewal and *Hurricane Center* returns always to the possibilities of redemption and joy.

In the voices of Jamaican prophets, Cuban exiles, drunks, race-track punters, canecutters, rastamen, middle-class householders and screw-face ghetto sufferers, Geoffrey Philp writes poetry which is both intimately human and cosmic in scale. On the airwaves between Miami and Kingston, the rhythms of reggae and mambo dance through these poems.

Geoffrey Philp was born in Jamaica. He now lives and works in Miami. He is the author of *Florida Bound* and a collection of short stories, *Uncle Obadiah and the Alien*, also published by Peepal Tree.

69 pages   £6.99   ISBN 1-900715-23-6   1998

Ralph Thompson

MOVING ON

The poems in *Moving On* recreate moments of change, loss and epiphany. There are vivid glimpses of a prewar Jamaican childhood – of sexual discovery under a billiard table and of the rude ingratitude of a goat saved from dissection in the school biology lab. The long sequence, 'Goodbye Aristotle, So Long America' explores the years of study at a Jesuit University in America and the making both of a lifetime's values and of the sense of irony which has made it possible to sustain them.

Other poems reflect on the experience of ageing, dealing not only with its increasing vulnerabilities, but also with its increased appreciation for what nurtures the survival of human relationships through time.

Jamaica is ever present in these poems, a place of aching natural beauty whose violent energies can only be viewed with an ambivalent love and fear, where:

In the city's bursting funeral parlours
the corpses glow at night, nimbus of blue
acetylene burning the darkness under the roof,
lighting the windows… crunch of bone and sinew
as a foot curls into a cloven hoof.

Louis Simpson described Ralph Thompson's first collection, also published by Peepal Tree, *The Denting of a Wave*, as "First rate poetry… intelligent and gifted with a sense of humour" and other reviewers praised its warmth, exact observation, craft and vivid story-telling. These qualities are present to an enhanced degree in *Moving On*.

Ralph Thompson is a Jamaican who, as well as being a painter and a poet, is the Senior Executive of on his country's biggest companies.

72 pages   £6.99   ISBN 1-900715-17-1   1998

Kwame Dawes

SHOOK FOIL

When the guitars tickle a bedrock of drum and bass, when the girl a shock out and a steady hand curve round her sweat-smooth waist, when the smell of *Charlie* mingles with the chemicals of her hair and the groove is of the sweetest friction... how is a young man to keep his way pure?

Kwame Dawes' poetry rises to new heights in these psalms of confession and celebrations of reggae's power to prophesy, to seek after righteousness and seduce the body and mind. Here is poetry walking the bassline, which darts sweetly around the rigid lick of the rhythm guitar yet expressing all the sadness and alienation at the heart of reggae. This, for Dawes, is the earth which 'never tells me my true home' and where behind every *chekeh* of the guitar there is the ancestral memory of the whip's crack.

Shook Foil dramatises the conflict between the purity of essences and the taints of the actual, not least in the poems which focus on Bob Marley's life. Here is the rhygin, word-weaving prophet *and* the philanderer with the desperate hunger for yard pumpum, the revealer of truths *and* the buffalo soldier who has married yard with show biz affluence.

Above all there is the intense sadness of Marley's death, for how can one live without the duppy conqueror's defiant wail in an island gone dark for the passing of his song?

But for *Shook Foil* there is always the gospeller's hope that the dead will rise from dub ruins and patch a new quilt of sound for the feet to prance on. And when the high hat shimmering and the bass drum thumping, what else to do but dance?

Kwame Dawes is the author of four other collections of poetry: *Progeny of Air*, *Prophets*, *Jacko Jacobus* and *Requiem*, published by Peepal Tree.

75 pages   £6.99   ISBN 1-900715-14-7   1997

Anthony McNeill

CHINESE LANTERNS FROM THE BLUE CHILD

> Somebody is hanging:
> a logwood tree
> laden with blossoms
> in a deep wood.
> The body stirs left
> in the wind;
> If the wind could send
> its miracle breath
> back to that person,
> I tell you it would.
> Love is Earth's mission
> despite the massed dead.
> On the night of the hanging
> the Autumn moon bled.

Anthony McNeill was without doubt amongst the finest contemporary Caribbean poets, whose previous collections, *Reel from 'The Life Movie'* and *Credences at the Altar of Cloud,* were hailed as works of immense originality. *Chinese Lanterns from the Blue Child* won the 1995 Jamaican National Literary Award. Completed shortly before his death, it is a farewell to the world which moves like a bird in flight between moments of painful regret, wry humour and a sense of closure.

Anthony McNeill's word-lanterns will continue to flame in the darkness long beyond his death. He was born in Jamaica in 1941. He died in 1996.

56 pages   £5.99   ISBN 1-900715-18-X   1998

Peepal Tree Press publishes a wide selection of outstanding fiction, poetry, drama, history and literary criticism with a focus on the Caribbean, Africa, the South Asian diaspora and Black life in Britain. Peepal Tree is now the largest independent publisher of Caribbean writing in the world. All our books are high quality original paperbacks designed to stand the test of time and repeated readings.

All Peepal Tree books should be available through your local bookseller, though you are most welcome to place orders direct with us. When ordering a book direct from us, simply tell us the title, author, quantity and the address to which the book should be mailed. Please enclose a cheque or money order for the cover price of the book, plus 75p towards postage and packing.

Peepal Tree produces a yearly catalogue which gives current prices in sterling, US and Canadian dollars and full details of all our books. Write, phone or fax for your free copy.

You can contact Peepal Tree direct at:

17 King's Avenue
Leeds LS6 1QS
United Kingdom

tel: 44 (0)113 245 1703
fax: 44 (0)113 246 8368
e-mail hannah@peepal.demon.co.uk